# LIVING ON PURPOSE

## DISCOVER YOUR PASSIONS, SET PURPOSEFUL GOALS, AND CULTIVATE A LIFE OF FULFILLMENT

Monika-om K

Copyright © 2024 Monika-om K

All rights reserved.

ISBN: 9798865326007

**Dear Reader,**

I trust this message finds you in good spirits as you delve into the pages of "Discover Your Life's Purpose: A Guide to Living Your Best Life." It's an honour to accompany you on this journey of self-discovery and personal growth.

Writing this book has been a labour of love, inspired by the belief that each individual possesses the power to craft a life filled with passion, purpose, and fulfilment. My sincere hope is that the words within these pages serve as a compass, guiding you towards a life that resonates with your deepest desires.

Your decision to explore the realms of life purpose and self-actualization is commendable, and I want to express my deepest gratitude for choosing this book as a companion on your path. As you navigate the chapters and engage with the exercises, remember that this is a shared exploration, and your insights and experiences are an integral part of the journey.

If you find value in the book or if certain sections resonate with you, I kindly invite you to share your feedback on Amazon. Your reviews are not only a source of encouragement for me but also invaluable insights for fellow seekers who might be contemplating the leap into discovering their purpose.

Your honest opinions contribute to the collective learning of our community, and your words may be the guiding light for someone embarking on this transformative journey.

Thank you once again for allowing "Discover Your Life's Purpose" into your life. May this book be a source of inspiration and empowerment as you uncover the extraordinary possibilities that await on your path to living your best life.

With heartfelt gratitude,

Monika-Om K

## Introduction

What does it mean to have the best life? In our busy modern world, it's easy to lose sight of what really matters. We go through each day on autopilot, without thinking deeply about what makes life truly worthwhile. But deep inside, there is a yearning for more - a life of passion, purpose, and fulfilment across all areas, including work, relationships, health, and personal growth.

The aim of this book is to provide clarity on how you can design and experience your version of the best life. While there is no one-size-fits-all solution, you'll discover techniques, tools, and mindsets to help you lead a meaningful and fulfilling existence on your own terms.

My goal is to distil the most resonant insights I've gathered over the years into an accessible guide. Consider me a fellow traveller hoping to provide a roadmap based on experience, introspection, and gleanings from many wise teachers. Together, we'll reflect, grow, and take consistent action so you can craft a deeply meaningful, joyful, and fulfilling life.

I don't have formal credentials as an author or expert. Like many, I've faced my share of adversity and struggles. I was at my lowest when I lost my first child in my mid-20s - life seemed utterly meaningless. During that painful period, I found hope by voraciously reading and examining the works of thinkers across fields like spirituality, psychology, health, and business. Their wisdom assisted me in getting back on my feet and aspiring to live a purposeful life.

# Disclaimer

**Legal Disclaimer:**

- This book is intended for informational and educational purposes only. It should not be considered professional advice. Consult a professional as needed for guidance on your specific situation.

- All rights are reserved by the author and/or publisher, and any unauthorized reproduction, distribution, or use is strictly prohibited.

- The author and publisher disclaim responsibility for any adverse effects resulting from the use or application of the information contained herein.

- Mention of third-party products, services, companies, or trademarks does not constitute endorsement or recommendation.

- The information provided is based on sources deemed reliable but cannot be guaranteed as error-free. It is provided as-is without warranty.

**Medical Disclaimer:**

- The information in this book related to health, wellness, and medical conditions is general in nature and should not be taken as medical advice or treatment recommendations. Consult your doctor before making any changes to your habits, diet, or lifestyle.

- The author does not diagnose, prescribe, or give medical advice. Do not disregard professional medical advice or delay seeking treatment based on anything herein.

**Financial Disclaimer:**

- The financial guidance provided is the author's opinion only. Results from taking any recommendations are not guaranteed. Conduct your own research before making investments or financial decisions.

- The author is not a licensed financial advisor or accountant. Consult a professional for customized guidance on your financial circumstances.

## CONTENTS

Introduction _____ iv
Disclaimer _____ v
CHAPTER 1: DISCOVER YOUR PASSIONS AND PURPOSE 1
CHAPTER 2: SET MEANINGFUL GOALS _____ 11
CHAPTER 3: CULTIVATE POSITIVE HABITS _____ 18
CHAPTER 4: FOSTER FULFILLING RELATIONSHIPS __ 27
CHAPTER 5: TAKE CARE OF YOUR HEALTH _____ 34
CHAPTER 6: MANAGE YOUR FINANCES WISELY _____ 40
CHAPTER 7: TRAVEL AND EXPAND YOUR HORIZONS 46
CHAPTER 8: MAKE TIME FOR WHAT MATTERS _____ 56
CHAPTER 9: DISCOVER WORK YOU LOVE _____ 61
CONCLUSION _____ 67
- The Final Thoughts _____ 74

# CHAPTER 1: DISCOVER YOUR PASSIONS AND PURPOSE

"The two most important days in your life are the day you are born and the day you find out why." – **Mark Twain**

Embarking on the journey to discover your life's purpose is like finding your voice—a rejuvenation, a rebirth, an experience akin to being alive once more. Life takes on profound meaning when you identify the core passions and purpose that ignite your spirit. This process of self-discovery is not just a quest; it's the very foundation upon which you'll build a life that resonates with your deepest desires.

Every successful person holds an abiding sense of purpose, similar to an unwavering dedication. Look around, the proof is evident. It's not necessarily about a grandiose objective or monumental ambition; it's about deriving joy from something meaningful. Whether it's volunteering at an animal shelter, stargazing, playing basketball, exploring marine life, developing apps, writing poetry, singing, painting, playing soccer, or gardening, the precise activity is insignificant. What matters is the ardent zeal that motivates their actions.

This enthusiasm becomes the driving force, keeping them captivated and engaged. It provides them with a profound sense of meaning, making them feel valued, purposeful, and deeply content. When motivated by passion and aligned aspirations, a deep sense of wholeness is felt. This inner fulfilment diminishes the sway of external factors. The serenity and joy stemming from within are not reliant on realizing a fixed goal; rather, they emerge from the knowledge that there's always something worthwhile to anticipate.

In this chapter, we embark on a journey within. I'll guide you through exercises, questions, and reflections meticulously designed to unveil what truly motivates you, what you hold most dear, and what imparts genuine meaning to your life.

**- Reflection exercises to get clarity on interests, values, passions**

In the quest to chart your course in life, it's imperative to gain a deep understanding of your current self before envisioning where you want to go. Let's embark on an introspective journey, delving beneath the surface layers of your identity.

**Unveiling Your Inner World: A Journey Back to Joy**

➢ **Memory Lane Exploration:**
**Childhood Joy Hunt:** Set a timer for 5 minutes and brainstorm moments from your childhood that brought you joy. What moments make you smile? Was it the splash of paint on canvas, the rhythm of dance, or the thrill of building things? Capture those joyous snippets of your past. Visualize and jot down your discoveries.

➢ **Role Model Reflection:**
**Admiration Unveiled:** To identify role models, ask yourself: Who do I admire and why? Jot down at least 3 figures who embody traits you aspire to? Your admiration often unveils aspects of your untapped potential. Share your reflections and let the discoveries inspire you.

➢ **Dreamland Vision:**
**Daydreaming Without Limits:** Imagine a world where time and money are no constraints. How would you spend your days? Envision your ideal life, highlighting the values that surface in your daydreams. Let this exercise illuminate the path to your authentic self.

**Ready to Dive In?**
**Use blank space in the book to record responses or keep a separate journal:**
➢ *Childhood Joy Moments: [Your Responses]*


➢ *Role Model Reflections: [Your Responses]*


➢ *Dreamland Vision: [Your Responses]*

By examining your past experiences, the people you look up to, and your ultimate fantasies, you reveal insights about your distinctive makeup.

**- Techniques to identify core strengths and talents**

Passion is enthusiasm so intense that it fuels personal growth and gives meaning to your life. Passions connect to your distinctive strengths, talents, and values.

Imagine you have a list of natural talents and potential strengths. Let's say your talents include creativity, analytical thinking, and communication. Now, cross-reference this list with activities that truly energize you and align with your core values. You discover that you thoroughly enjoy graphic design, problem-solving through coding, and public speaking about social issues.

The intersecting points between your talents and energizing activities become a roadmap, signaling possible passions. Now, let's ask a few crucial questions

> ➢ **Does graphic design, a blend of creativity and analytical thinking, hold your attention for hours of focus and practice?** If the answer is a resounding yes, it indicates a strong alignment between your talent and passion.

> ➢ **Do you find yourself repeatedly telling stories or discussing concepts related to coding and problem-solving?** If this activity becomes a natural part of your conversations, it suggests a deep connection and enthusiasm.

> ➢ **Can you envision yourself excelling and making a difference by addressing social issues through public speaking?** If you feel a sense of purpose and impact in this domain, it points towards a passion that aligns with your values.

Once you've pondered these questions and pinpointed your passions using this cross-referencing technique, they become the North Star guiding you towards fulfilment. Just like a compass that consistently points to the North, your passions will consistently guide your decisions and actions on the path to a more fulfilling and purpose-driven life.

## - Tips for brainstorming life purposes aligned with passion

Your life purpose weaves together your core passions and values with a vision for how to apply them for good. Reflect on these questions to decipher your purpose:

> ➤ **Strengthening the World:**

**Utilizing Your Powers:** Reflect on your strengths and passions. How can you leverage these unique qualities to make a positive impact on others or society at large? Share your thoughts on the endless possibilities that arise when personal strengths meet societal needs.

> ➤ **Crafting Your Legacy:**

**Leaving a Mark:** Consider the legacy you wish to leave behind in the world. What impact do you aspire to make? Delve into your vision for a lasting imprint, whether it's through meaningful relationships, societal contributions, or transformative initiatives.

> ➤ **Fearless Dreaming:**

**If Failure Were Impossible:** Imagine a realm where failure is not an option. What daring dreams would you pursue with unwavering determination? Envision the boundless potential of your aspirations, unrestricted by the fear of setbacks.

**Share Your Vision Below or on a separate journal:**

> *Strengthening the World: [Your Responses]*

> *Crafting Your Legacy: [Your Responses]*

> *Fearless Dreaming: [Your Responses]*

Your answers assemble into a central purpose – the lighthouse guiding your choices and goals. Staying true to this purpose will enable living your best life.

Here's an example of the cross-referencing technique:

| Natural Talents | Energizing Activities | Passions |
|---|---|---|
| Creativity | Graphic Design | Passion 1 |
| Analytical Thinking | Coding/Problem-solving | Passion 2 |
| Communication | Public Speaking | Passion 3 |

In this representation:

*"Natural Talents"* are listed on the left.

*"Energizing Activities"* are in the middle.

*"Passions"* are on the right, indicating the intersections between talents and activities.

The journey of self-discovery never truly ends. But unearthing your passions and purpose equips you with the compass needed to orient your best life path.

**- Case studies of others who have found their purpose**
In the realm of personal and professional development, real-life experiences often serve as invaluable lessons, offering

insights into challenges faced, decisions made, and the transformative outcomes that ensued. This collection presents two compelling case studies, each unraveling a distinct narrative of resilience, innovation, and growth. From a talented creative soul who pivoted from a conventional career to embrace entrepreneurship, to the inspiring story of a single mother who, without a grand purpose in sight, dedicated her life in service to humanity — these case studies exemplify the diverse paths one can tread in the pursuit of a meaningful and fulfilling life. Join us on a journey through the intricacies of these narratives, discovering the lessons embedded within the fabric of real-life endeavours.

## Case Study 1: From Law School to Flourishing Entrepreneur: Siya's Journey into Makeup Artistry:

Meet Siya, a talented and creative individual who, despite excelling in law school and obtaining a law degree, discovered her true passion lay in the world of makeup artistry. Her journey is a compelling case study on how finding one's purpose can lead to unexpected, yet fulfilling, career paths. What makes Siya's story even more relatable is that she was a school friend, someone whose transformation we witnessed firsthand.

### Background:
Siya displayed a flair for creativity since her early school days. Her artistic talents stood out, and many of us believed she would pursue a career in the arts. However, she chose a more conventional path and decided to study law at university, earning her degree with distinction.

**Transition to Law:**
After graduation, Siya began practicing law, working for a reputable firm. She found success in her legal career, but over time, a lingering sense of unfulfillment crept in. Despite her achievements in law, Siya felt a void, a yearning for something that would ignite her creative spirit.

**Discovering the Passion:**
In her pursuit of personal fulfillment, Siya explored her long-lost passion for makeup artistry. What started as a hobby soon became a burning desire to turn her creative skills into a profession. Siya, our dear school friend, made the courageous decision to step away from her legal career and embark on a new journey.

**Entrepreneurial Leap:**
Siya's transition to becoming a makeup artist wasn't without challenges. However, armed with determination and a keen eye for artistic details, she started her own makeup business. The entrepreneurial leap came with risks, but Siya's passion and commitment fueled her drive.

**The Business Blooms:**
To her surprise and delight, Siya's makeup artistry business flourished. Her unique approach, blending legal precision with artistic flair, resonated with clients seeking distinctive and personalized makeup experiences. Word of mouth spread, and soon, Siya found herself fully booked with appointments.

**Overcoming Challenges:**

While the path to entrepreneurship had its hurdles, Siya embraced challenges as learning opportunities. From managing finances to marketing her brand, she navigated the complexities of running a business, all while staying true to her creative roots.

**Conclusion:**
Siya's case study is a testament to the transformative power of pursuing one's true calling. From being a successful law professional to becoming a thriving makeup artist and business owner, her story, as a school friend, inspires us all to listen to our passions and take bold steps toward a purposeful life.

## Case Study 2: The Compassionate Journey: A Case Study on My Grandmother's Selfless Dedication as a Single Mother

This case study sheds light on the inspiring life of my grandmother, a remarkable woman who, without any grand purpose, dedicated her life to raising two children as a single mother. Her story is a testament to the profound impact one person's compassionate service can have on the lives of others.

**Background:**
Growing up in a time when societal norms were vastly different, my grandmother found herself thrust into the role of a single mother. With no grand purpose in mind, she embraced her responsibility with unwavering dedication and a heart full of compassion.

**Single Motherhood:**
Facing the challenges of single motherhood, my grandmother focused on creating a nurturing environment for her two children. Despite the absence of a grand plan, her daily acts of love, sacrifice, and resilience laid the foundation for a home filled with warmth and understanding.

**Dedication to Service:**
What makes my grandmother's story remarkable is her dedication to service. Without the grandest of purposes, she selflessly devoted her life to ensuring her children had the best opportunities available. Her service was not just within the confines of her home but extended to the community, creating a ripple effect of kindness and compassion.

**Compassion in Action:**
My grandmother's compassionate nature wasn't limited to her immediate family. She actively participated in community service, offering support to neighbors, friends, and anyone in need. Her small acts of kindness, though not driven by a grand purpose, had a profound impact on those around her.

**Impact on the Children:**
The love and compassion my grandmother poured into her children's lives formed a solid foundation for their growth. Despite the absence of a grand plan, she instilled in them values of kindness, empathy, and the importance of serving others.

**Legacy of Compassion:**
As her grandchildren, we are a living testament to the

legacy of compassion my grandmother cultivated. Her selfless dedication, though seemingly without a grand purpose, has created a lasting impact on generations.

**Conclusion:**

My grandmother's case study illuminates the power of compassion and service, even when driven by a seemingly simple purpose. Her life exemplifies the profound effect one person can have on the world by approaching each day with a heart full of love and a commitment to making a difference, one small act at a time.

# CHAPTER 2: SET MEANINGFUL GOALS

Once you have clarity on your core passions and purpose, the next step is setting goals that align with them. Goals give direction and a sense of meaning to day-to-day life. They stretch your capabilities and enable accomplishment. This chapter reveals how to set impactful goals and actually achieve them.

**- Difference between goals and aspirations**
It's important to distinguish goals from mere aspirations. An aspiration is a hope or desire, like "I want to travel the world." A goal is a specific, measurable target that stretches you such as "I will visit 10 new countries in the next 5 years." Aspirations state a wish, whereas proper goals outline the tangible steps to fulfil it.

- Creating S.M.A.R.T. goals with specific measurable targets
The most effective goals adhere to the S.M.A.R.T. framework:

| | Creating S.M.A.R.T. Goals |
|---|---|
| Specific | Well defined, with a clear expected outcome.<br><br>**Specific Details**<br>Define specific areas of improvement, such as mastering advanced Photoshop techniques. |
| Measurable | Quantifiable targets to track progress.<br><br>**Measurable Targets**<br>Achieve a 20% increase in project completion speed within the next three |

|   |   |
|---|---|
| Achievable | months. Within reach if you stretch yourself<br><br>**Achievable Actions**<br>Enroll in an advanced graphic design course. Practice new techniques for at least 1 hour daily. |
| Relevant | Aligns with other goals and larger purpose<br><br>**Relevance to Goals**<br>Enhances skill set for career advancement. |
| Time-bound | With set deadlines for completion<br><br>**Time-bound Deadlines**<br>Complete the graphic design course in the next six weeks. |

- Setting goals in key categories: career, financial, education, health, relationships, personal growth

Embarking on your journey to your best life involves setting S.M.A.R.T. goals across vital life categories. Consider the following potential goal areas as your compass:

> **Career**:
> - Example Goal: Achieve promotion to Senior Manager within the next 12 months.

> **Financial**:
> - Example Goal: Save $4000 this year, earmarked

for an unforgettable vacation fund.

- **Education:**
  - Example Goal: Enroll in a photography course by the third quarter of 2024.

- **Health:**
  - Example Goal: Shed 10lbs by the end of the year for a healthier you.

- **Relationships:**
  - Example Goal: Foster connection by scheduling biweekly date nights with your spouse.

- **Personal Growth:**
  - Example Goal: Cultivate self-reflection with a daily 5-minute journaling practice.

Crafting S.M.A.R.T. goals is more than a strategy—it's your personalized roadmap to living your best life. Keep the momentum alive by regularly tracking your progress, celebrating achievements, and adjusting course as needed. Your journey to success begins with intentional, measurable steps.

**- Evaluating and adjusting goals over time**
As you navigate your journey towards your best life, it's crucial to revisit your goals regularly. Use this reflective checklist to ensure your goals remain in harmony with your evolving self:

- **Alignment with Core Values and Purpose:**
    - Are my goals still aligned with my core values and life purpose?
    - Ensure that your aspirations resonate with the principles and purpose that guide your journey.
- **Relevance amid Life Changes:**
    - Have some goals become irrelevant based on recent life changes?
    - Acknowledge shifts in circumstances and realign goals to match your current reality.
- **Balancing Priorities:**
    - Do my priorities need rebalancing?
    - Evaluate if adjustments are necessary to maintain a harmonious balance across various life dimensions.
- **Inspiration and Challenge:**
    - Are my goals still inspiring and challenging enough?
    - Ensure that your goals ignite passion and push you to grow, remaining compelling on your journey.

Your goals are not static; they evolve with you. Regular reflection ensures that your aspirations continue to serve as beacons, guiding you towards a life that aligns with your deepest desires. Embrace change, celebrate growth, and let your goals evolve in tandem with your extraordinary journey.

Keep nurturing your dreams and reflecting on your path—your best life is an ever-unfolding masterpiece.

**- Navigating Obstacles on the Path**
The path to any worthy goal has hurdles. Anticipate challenges and develop strategies to overcome them. Common obstacles include:

> **Lack of motivation** - Revisit why the goal matters. Consider benefits achieved by progress made so far. Connect goals to your core values and purpose for renewed inspiration.

**Example**: Imagine you set a goal to exercise regularly, but after a few weeks, you find yourself lacking motivation. Revisit why exercising matters to you – it could be for better health, increased energy, or stress relief. Consider the benefits you've experienced so far, like improved mood or increased stamina. Connect these goals to your core values, such as the value you place on your well-being or your desire to be present for your family. By aligning your goals with your values, you can find renewed inspiration to stay committed to your exercise routine.

> **Competing priorities** - If goals conflict, re-evaluate importance and necessity. Eliminate goals diverting focus from your highest priorities. Schedule daily time protecting priority goals.

**Example**: If you set a goal to advance in your career but find competing priorities with family obligations, re-evaluate the importance and necessity of each goal. Determine your highest priorities and eliminate goals that divert your focus. If career advancement aligns with your highest priorities, schedule dedicated daily time for work-related tasks. By protecting priority goals with a set schedule, you can strike a balance and prevent competing priorities from derailing your progress.

➢ **Lack of skills/knowledge** - Determine expertise needed to achieve the goal. Enrol in courses, get a mentor, or gain hands-on experience. Invest time upfront in acquiring required abilities.

**Example**: Suppose your goal is to start a small business, but you lack the necessary skills in marketing. Determine the expertise needed for your goal – in this case, marketing skills. Enroll in relevant courses, seek guidance from a mentor, or gain hands-on experience through online projects. Invest time upfront in acquiring the required abilities, understanding that building these skills is an essential step toward achieving your business goals.

➢ **Fear of failure** - View setbacks as learning experiences, not endpoints. Consider what went wrong and course correct. Believe in your capacity to eventually succeed.

**Example**: You aspire to write a novel but are held back by the fear of failure. Instead of viewing setbacks as endpoints, consider them as learning experiences. If a particular chapter doesn't work, analyze what went wrong and course-correct. Remind yourself of successful authors who faced rejection before achieving recognition. Believe in your capacity to learn and grow through the process, understanding that each setback is a stepping stone toward eventual success.

➢ Stay resilient by proactively planning for hurdles. Tap into your deepest motivations and commit to acquiring skills incrementally. With grit and perseverance, obstacles morph into stepping stones.

**Example**: In pursuing a fitness goal, you encounter unexpected hurdles like injuries or time constraints. Stay resilient by proactively planning for these obstacles. Tap into your deepest motivations for fitness – whether it's improving health or setting an example for your children. Commit to acquiring skills incrementally, such as learning about injury prevention or finding time-efficient workouts. With grit and perseverance, what initially seemed like obstacles will transform into stepping stones on your fitness journey.

To see perseverance in action, let me share my Brother Jack's inspiring tale of grit on his marathon quest...

In his Early-thirties, Jack decided to take up running to improve his health. He started small, just running a few miles per week. Eventually, he set the lofty goal of finishing a marathon within a year.

Initially, the training went smoothly. He was steadily increasing mileage and meeting target times. But close to race day, Jack hit a major roadblock. During a 20-mile training run, he injured his knee badly. The doctor advised taking a long break from running.

Jack was crushed. His marathon dream seemed impossible now. Still, he refused to give up entirely. He cross-trained to maintain fitness. After nearly 2 months, he was able to run again with minimal pain. However, by now he had missed so much training that finishing a marathon in the original timeframe was unrealistic.

But Jack was stubborn in the best way. He modified his goal to accommodate the setback. He spent another 8 months slowly building back mileage and endurance.

Finally, over 2 years after initially setting the goal, Jack proudly completed his first marathon. Crossing the finish line brought him to tears after defying massive obstacles.

Jack's perseverance teaches us an important lesson - with enough determination, you can still accomplish ambitious goals despite major setbacks on the journey. When challenges arise, take time to heal and modify your plan, but keep inching towards your aim. With relentless tenacity and inner resolve, your vision can become reality even if the road is winding.

## CHAPTER 3: CULTIVATE POSITIVE HABITS

Transforming your lifestyle to align with your passions and purpose requires developing supportive daily habits. The right small habits compound over time into remarkable results.

The power of habits stems from their compounding effects over time. With consistency, even modest positive habits create seismic impact as the benefits accumulate.

For example, reading 20 pages daily translates into 7300 pages completed in a year. Walking 30 minutes daily equates to 182 hours of exercise over 6 months. Meditating 5 minutes daily provides 30 hours of mindfulness over the course of a year.

Like interest growing exponentially in savings, the returns from tiny habits multiply substantially. The 3% lifestyle inflation from an extra 20 minutes of television daily equals 120 hours wasted in a year. But 3% self-improvement from a 20 minute daily walk yields monumental dividends for your health long-term.

**Atomic habits expert James Clear explains this math powerfully:**

"The difference a tiny improvement can make over time is astounding. Here is an example: if you can get just 1 percent better each day for one year, you'll end up thirty-seven times better by the time you're done. Conversely, if you get 1 percent worse each day for one year, you'll decline nearly down to zero."

The chapter provides an overview of habit development with specific examples and techniques that bolster your best life.

**- Habits that lead to success like consistency, discipline, learning**

Achieving any worthy goal demands consistency in small actions. Like compound interest, the effects of positive habits accumulate dramatically over weeks, months, and years. Regular exercise for 20 minutes makes you far healthier than sporadic 2-hour sessions.

Do not underestimate the potential of micro-improvements through atomic habits aligned with your purpose. They set in motion lifelong positive momentum. With grit and discipline, you begin actualizing your best life.

Building an ideal daily routine is the key to sculpting the life you desire. Tailor your day to embrace the following priorities, converting them into steadfast habits that foster growth, connection, and well-being:

- **Learning**
  - **Habit: Read 20 pages daily**
    Dedicate time to expanding your knowledge through literature, ensuring a daily commitment to lifelong learning.

- Relationships:
  - **Habit: Share appreciation with a loved one nightly**
    Cultivate connection by expressing gratitude and appreciation, nurturing the bonds that matter most.

- Health:
  - **Habit: Walk 30 minutes every morning**
    Prioritize your physical well-being with a morning walk, kick-starting your day with movement and fresh air.

- Personal Growth:
  - **Habit: Journal 5 minutes to reflect**
    Carve out a brief moment for self-reflection, fostering personal growth and mindfulness through daily journaling.

- Recreation:
  - **Habit: Limit social media to 30 minutes daily**
    Consciously manage screen time, ensuring a healthy balance between digital engagement and real-world experiences.

### -The Power of Consistency

Even the most modest habits, when practiced consistently, have the potential to create a seismic impact over time. Your daily routine serves as a canvas, allowing you to paint a life rich in purpose, connection, and well-being. Embrace these habits as the building blocks of your extraordinary journey—one day at a time.

### - Reducing unproductive habits like distraction and procrastination

Just as valuable habits enable your purpose, limiting unproductive ones prevents distraction. Common time-wasters include internet surfing, excessive social media, pointless Smartphone use, random YouTube/Netflix viewing.

Leverage mindfulness to become aware of unfulfilling habits. Note triggers causing you to veer off track. Then consciously decide to eliminate or reduce that habit. If you want to maintain the habit but control its impact, impose constraints like allowing only at set times or for fixed duration.

- **Specific techniques for habit formation like accountability partners, rewards**

Enlist friends or an accountability partner to reinforce forming new, positive habits. Share your goals and schedule periodic check-ins on progress. Accountability helps ingrain habits through motivation and peer support.

Also utilize tracking apps or a habit journal to monitor consistency. Record daily progress and chart milestones reached. Visible progress builds momentum. Reward successes to further positive reinforcement.

Life-changing transformation happens gradually through small habit formation.

Consistently practice a few positive habits aligned to your purpose and watch their compounding over months and years.

- **Morning and evening rituals for self-improvement**

Transform your mornings into a sanctuary of self-improvement with this invigorating ritual. Infuse each moment with intention, mindfulness, and positive energy for a day that aligns with your highest aspirations:

➤ **Early Awakening:**
  - **Habit**: Wake up early and drink warm lemon water

Greet the day with hydration and revitalization, setting the stage for a mindful morning.

- ➢ **Breath Awareness Meditation:**
    - **Practice**: 10 minutes of breath awareness meditation
    Center yourself through intentional breath, fostering clarity and calmness for the day ahead.

- ➢ **Mantras for Empowerment:**
    - **Chant**: Uplifting mantras like "I am strong, healthy, and filled with energy"
    Infuse your being with positivity and strength through empowering affirmations.

- ➢ **Energizing Breath Techniques:**
    - **Try**: 5 rounds of Kapalabhati & Bhastrika breath techniques
    Stimulate vitality and energy with invigorating breathwork techniques.

- ➢ **Gratitude Journaling:**
    - **Habit**: Write in a gratitude journal - list 3 things you're thankful for
    Ground yourself in appreciation, fostering a mindset of gratitude.

➢ **Mindful Movement:**
  - **Exercise**: Take a short walk, do yoga/stretches, or a bodyweight workout
  Activate your body and mind, promoting physical well-being and mental clarity.

➢ **Nourishing Breakfast:**
  - **Habit**: Make and enjoy a nourishing breakfast
  Fuel your body with wholesome goodness, providing energy for the day.

➢ **Inspirational Reading:**
  - **Read**: Inspirational text like spiritual quotes to set intention for the day
  Commence your day with wisdom, aligning your intentions with uplifting thoughts.

➢ **Embrace the Art of Mindful Mornings**
  - This morning ritual transcends routine—it's a symphony of mindful practices harmonizing to elevate your mind, body, and spirit. Infuse your mornings with this transformative rhythm, and watch as each day unfolds as a canvas of self-improvement and purpose.

➢ **Unwind with an Evening Ritual**
  - Cultivate tranquility and reflection with this rejuvenating evening ritual. Let each element guide you into a restful night, promoting mental clarity and a sense of inner peace.

- **Mindful Dining:**
  - **Practice**: Mindfulness during dinner - slow down and savor the food
  - Transform your mealtime into a mindful experience, savouring each bite with gratitude.

- **Relaxing Hygiene Routine:**
  - **Habit**: Take a relaxing warm bath or shower
  Rinse away the day's tensions, preparing your body and mind for rest.

- **Restorative Yoga and Stretches:**
  - **Try**: Restorative yoga poses or gentle body stretches
  Release physical tension and invite relaxation through gentle movements.

- **Evening Meditation:**
  - **Meditate**: 15 minutes - focusing on breath or body scan
  Calm your mind and promote inner peace through guided meditation.

- **Calming Pranayama:**
  - **Do**: 5 rounds of Nadi Shodhana alternate nostril breathing
  Enhance relaxation with soothing pranayama, syncing breath and balance.

> **Ambient Sounds or Silence:**
>   - **Listen**: To soft music or sit in silence
>     Create a tranquil ambiance, allowing your mind to unwind.

> **Reflective Journaling:**
>   - **Reflect**: In a journal - write about your day, lessons learned, feelings
>   - Process your day's experiences, fostering self-awareness and emotional release.

> **Gratitude and Accomplishments:**
>   - **Write**: 3 things you're grateful for and 1 accomplishment from the day
>     Cultivate gratitude and acknowledge your achievements, promoting a positive mindset.

> **Positive Visualization:**
>   - **Practice**: Positive self-talk and visualize your goals before bed
>     Guide your mind towards positivity, reinforcing your aspirations.

Consistency is the key to this evening ritual's magic. As you weave these practices into your nightly routine, watch as they collectively contribute to elevating your physical health, mental clarity, and overall well-being. Embrace the tranquility and self-care that each evening brings, paving the way for restful nights and inspired days.

## CHAPTER 4: FOSTER FULFILLING RELATIONSHIPS

Humans are social beings – finding meaning, joy, and purpose through connections. But in modern life's hustle, relationships often get neglected. Nurturing your most vital bonds is crucial for living your best life. This chapter reveals how to foster relationships that lift you higher.

**Nurturing Meaningful Connections: A Strategic Approach**

Time is a precious resource, and investing it wisely in relationships can profoundly impact your life. Here's a strategic guide to identifying relationships that deserve your valuable time and attention:

- **Family Bonds:**
  - **Consider:** Close family who have always supported you.
  Prioritize relationships with family members whose unwavering support has been a constant in your life.

- **Growth-Oriented Friendships:**
  - **Focus on:** Friends who inspire personal growth
  Channel your energy into friendships that uplift and contribute to your personal development.

- **Wisdom-Seeking Mentors:**
  - **Engage with:** Mentors who share wisdom and advice.
  Cultivate relationships with mentors, whose insights align with your goals, providing valuable guidance.

- **Aligned Communities:**
  - **Join:** Groups that share your values and interests
  Connect with communities where shared values and interests foster a sense of belonging and mutual growth.

By deliberately choosing where to invest your time and emotional energy, you create a network of relationships that enrich your life. Focus on those who have consistently supported you, inspire personal growth, share valuable wisdom, and align with your core values. In doing so, you build a foundation of meaningful connections that contribute to your well-being and personal development.

## - Relationship Evaluation and Strengthening Blueprint

Building and maintaining meaningful connections require thoughtful evaluation and intentional effort. Here's a blueprint to assess and strengthen your relationships:

### Evaluation Criteria:
- **History:**
  - **Assess**: Evaluate the depth of your shared history and experiences.
  
  **Action**: Prioritize relationships with a rich history that holds sentimental value.

- **Positivity:**
  - **Reflect on:** The overall positivity and joy in the relationship.
  
  **Action**: Invest in relationships that consistently bring joy and positivity to your life.

- **Meaning:**
  - **Consider**: How meaningful and purpose-driven is the relationship?
  
  **Action**: Prioritize connections that align with your values and contribute to your sense of purpose.

- **Fun:**
  - **Evaluate**: The element of fun and enjoyment in your interactions.
  
  **Action**: Foster relationships that bring joy and create enjoyable memories.

- **Inspiration:**
  - **Reflect on:** How the relationship inspires personal and collective growth.
  - **Action:** Invest in connections that inspire and contribute to mutual development.

**Strengthening Techniques:**

- **Quality Time:**
  - **Engage in:** Make quality time for substantive communication.
  - **Result:** Deepen connections through meaningful conversations.

- **Full Presence:**
  - **Practice:** Be fully present and actively listen without distractions.
  - **Result:** Cultivate a deeper understanding and connection.

- **Acts of Care:**
  - **Express:** Show care through actions like a handwritten letter or a thoughtful gesture.
  - **Result:** Create a tangible expression of your appreciation.

- **Personal Sharing:**
  - **Engage in:** Share personally to become more vulnerable and intimate.
  - **Result:** Foster a sense of trust and intimacy in the relationship.

> **Acknowledgment:**
- **Offer:** Compliment them on how they've positively impacted you.
  **Result:** Reinforce the positive aspects of the relationship.

  Small, intentional gestures and shared meaningful experiences contribute to the depth and strength of relationships. Assess your connections, invest in those aligned with your well-being, and nurture them through thoughtful actions.

**- Effective communication techniques to prevent misunderstanding**

Effective communication is the cornerstone of meaningful connections. Incorporate these practices into your conversations for more impactful and empathetic communication:

> **Avoiding Multitasking:**
  **Practice:** Dedicate your full attention to the person you're conversing with.
  **Result:** Deepen understanding and demonstrate respect for their thoughts.

> **Clarifying Intent:**
  **Initiate by:** Clearly stating your intent before important conversations.
  **Result:** Set the right tone and expectations for the discussion.

> **Restating Key Points:**
**Demonstrate**: Confirm your understanding by restating key points they made.
**Result**: Minimize misunderstandings and reinforce active listening.

> **Discussing Difficult Issues:**
**Approach**: Engage in difficult conversations respectfully, without judgment.
**Result**: Create a safe space for open dialogue and understanding.

> **Active Listening:**
**Practice**: Hear them out before responding to their statements.
**Result**: Foster a culture of respect and encourage the expression of diverse perspectives.

> **Empathy:**
**Infuse**: Bridge gaps in understanding with empathy.
**Result**: Strengthen emotional connections and foster a supportive environment.

Effective communication is not just about conveying information; it's about creating an atmosphere of understanding, respect, and empathy. By incorporating these practices, you contribute to building stronger, more meaningful relationships.

## ➢ Navigating Relationship Conflicts

In the intricate dance of relationships, conflicts are an inevitable part of the journey. However, the key lies in managing these conflicts constructively. Here are strategies to prevent lasting damage and foster understanding:

➢ **Addressing Issues Early:**
**Anticipate**: Tackle issues at their onset, preventing escalation.
**Result**: Maintain a healthier and more communicative dynamic.

➢ **Finding Common Ground:**

**Emphasize**: Communicate shared goals, reaffirming you're on the same team.
**Result**: Reinforce unity, emphasizing collaboration over opposition.

➢ **Taking Time to Cool Off:**
**Practice**: When emotions run high, take a step back for perspective.
**Result**: Avoid saying things in the heat of the moment that may cause lasting harm.

➢ **Compromising with Cooperation:**
**Approach**: Enter conflicts with a cooperative, non-adversarial mindset.
**Result**: Reach solutions that benefit both parties, nurturing mutual understanding.

Preserving the bonds that matter involves conflict

resolution focused on mutual comprehension. While relationships demand ongoing care and attention, the meaning and joy they bring make the effort profoundly rewarding. Prioritize the cultivation of your most uplifting connections for a fulfilling journey together.

- **Creating new meaningful connections**

In the tapestry of life, new relationships are like vibrant threads weaving in fresh experiences and perspectives. Here are some proactive ways to connect with like-minded individuals and nurture these budding connections:

➢ **Take Classes and Volunteer:**
  - **Explore Interests:** Enroll in classes or volunteer for causes aligned with your passions.
  - **Result:** Build connections through shared interests and common pursuits.

➢ **Join Clubs or Community Groups:**
  - **Community Engagement:** Become part of clubs or groups related to hobbies like hiking, reading, or photography.
  - **Result:** Foster connections in a setting that encourages shared activities.

➢ **Attend Networking Events:**
  - **Professional Networks:** Engage in industry events or conferences.
  - **Result:** Connect with individuals who share your professional aspirations.

- ➤ **Explore Spiritual Communities:**
  - **Spiritual Growth:** Participate in activities at places of worship.
  - **Result:** Bond with individuals who share similar spiritual values.

- ➤ **Try Team Sports:**
  - **Athletic Pursuits:** Join team sport leagues.
  - **Result:** Forge bonds while enjoying physical activities together.

Initiate meaningful conversations by delving into others' interests, values, and passions. Actively listen, seeking common ground, and follow up to nurture promising connections. Meaningful relationships blossom when you invest time, genuine interest, and care. Remember, each new connection holds the potential for enrichment and joy.

Taking initiative to encounter like-minded individuals, combined with selective investment of time and energy, ensures a gradual and fulfilling expansion of your social circle.

## CHAPTER 5: TAKE CARE OF YOUR HEALTH

*"To keep the body in good health is a duty...otherwise we shall not be able to keep our mind strong and clear." – Buddha*

Your health span – not just lifespan – enables fulfilling pursuits. Optimizing your wellbeing boosts energy, outlook, and enjoyment of life. This chapter reveals how to incorporate nutrition, fitness, sleep, and stress management into a thriving lifestyle.

### - Fundamentals of nutrition and meal planning

Embarking on your journey towards your best life involves recognizing the profound impact of nutrition on your wellbeing. Here are fundamental principles to guide your approach to healthy eating:

➢ **Embrace Wholesome Foods:**

- **Prioritize Nutrient-Rich Choices:** Focus on vegetables, fruits, whole grains, lean protein, and healthy fats.
- **Result:** Nourish your body with essential vitamins and minerals for optimal functioning.

➢ **Limit Processed Foods:**

- **Reduce Culprits:** Minimize consumption of processed foods, salt, sugar, saturated fats, and fast food.
- **Result:** Promote overall health and reduce the risk of chronic diseases.

- **Hydrate for Vitality:**

  - **Water is Life:** Ensure adequate hydration by drinking sufficient water daily.
  - **Result:** Support bodily functions, enhance energy levels, and maintain clear mental focus.

- **Culinary Mastery at Home:**

  - **Cook with Love:** Learn to prepare simple, nutritious meals at home.
  - **Result:** Foster a deeper connection with your food, ensuring wholesome and mindful consumption.

- **Balanced Indulgence:**

  - **Occasional Treats:** Allow yourself occasional indulgences in moderation without guilt.
  - **Result:** Strike a balance between pleasure and nutrition.

- **Supplement Smartly:**

  - **Cover Nutritional Bases:** Consider taking a quality multivitamin to ensure comprehensive nutrition.
  - **Result:** Safeguard against potential deficiencies for overall well-being.

Remember, proper nutrition serves as the cornerstone for elevated energy levels, mental clarity, strengthened immunity, and sustained overall health. By making informed choices in your diet, you lay the foundation for a vibrant and fulfilling life.

**- Developing exercise habits and fitness plans**

In the pursuit of your best life, establishing a consistent exercise routine is as crucial as maintaining a wholesome diet. Here are key principles to guide your journey to a more active and vibrant lifestyle:

➢ **Commit to Consistency:**
- **150 Minutes Weekly:** Aim for at least 150 minutes per week of moderate activity, such as brisk walking.
- **Result:** Enhance cardiovascular health and overall well-being.

➢ **Strength for Resilience:**
- **Muscle-Strengthening Sessions:** Engage in strength training 2-3 times a week to build and tone muscles.
- **Result:** Improve muscle mass, metabolism, and overall body strength.

➢ **Daily Movement Ritual:**
- **Stay Active Daily:** Incorporate some form of physical activity into your daily routine, even a short walk around the block.
- **Result:** Boost energy, mood, and maintain agility.

➢ **Diverse Exercise Regimen:**
- **Mix It Up:** Include a blend of cardiovascular exercises,

strength training, and flexibility routines.
- **Result**: Holistic fitness, addressing different aspects of physical health.

➢ **Find Joy in Activity:**
- **Explore Enjoyable Pursuits:** Integrate activities you love, be it sports, swimming, hiking, or any form of exercise that brings joy.
- **Result**: Foster a positive relationship with physical activity for sustained engagement.

Remember, movement is the key to maintaining the agility of both body and mind. Start your fitness journey from your current point, gradually increasing intensity and duration. With commitment and gradual progress, you'll discover the transformative power of an active lifestyle.

### - Ensuring sufficient sleep quantity and quality

In the quest for your best life, don't underestimate the profound impact of quality sleep on your overall well-being. Here are some tried-and-true practices to ensure restorative and rejuvenating sleep:

➢ **Consistency is Key:**
- **Set a Schedule:** Maintain a consistent sleep-wake schedule, even on weekends, to regulate your body's internal clock.
- **Result**: Improved sleep quality and overall circadian rhythm.

- Dim the Lights:

  - **Limit Blue Light:** Minimize exposure to blue light from devices before bedtime; it interferes with melatonin production.
  - **Result:** Easier transition into a restful state.

- Create an Oasis of Rest:

  - **Optimize Sleep Environment:** Ensure your sleep space is cool, dark, and quiet, fostering an ideal setting for relaxation.
  - **Result:** Enhanced sleep quality and duration.

- Mindful Pre-Sleep Routine:

  - **Unplug and Unwind:** Avoid stimulation, big meals, and vigorous exercise within 1-2 hours of bedtime.
  - **Result:** A calmer mind and body conducive to sleep.

- Soothing Nighttime Rituals:

  - **Relaxing Activities**: Engage in activities like journaling, light reading, or meditation to calm your mind.
  - **Result:** Improved mental tranquility for a smoother transition to sleep.

- **Prioritize Sleep Duration:**
  - **Aim for 7-9 Hours:** Target 7-9 hours of sleep nightly for optimal physical and mental restoration.
  - **Result:** Improved concentration, mood, and immune function.

Remember, time spent in bed is an investment in your overall well-being. By adopting these sleep practices, you empower your body and mind to thrive, ensuring you wake up each day ready to embrace life's opportunities with vitality and vigor.

- Stress management through mindfulness, nature, socializing

In the pursuit of your best life, managing stress is not just a choice; it's a necessity. Here are some effective strategies to counteract stress and foster well-being:

- **Mindfulness Mastery:**
  - **Daily Mindfulness Practices:** Integrate meditation, yoga, or breathwork into your daily routine to cultivate resilience.
  - **Result:** Enhanced emotional balance and a centered state of mind.

- **Social Wellness Boost:**
  - **Social Interaction:** Actively engage in social activities throughout the week to strengthen your support network.
  - **Result:** Building resilience through

meaningful connections.

- ➤ **Nature's Healing Touch:**
    - **Embrace Nature:** Immerse yourself in the calming benefits of nature through activities like hiking, gardening, or simply spending time outdoors.
    - **Result**: Reduced stress levels and increased overall well-being.

- ➤ **Boundaries for Balance:**
    - **Set Boundaries:** Learn to say no and establish clear boundaries to prevent burnout and protect your mental health.
    - **Result**: Maintaining a healthy work-life balance and avoiding overwhelm.

- ➤ **Thought Reframing:**
    - **Challenge Negative Thoughts:** Reframe anxiety-provoking thoughts by adopting a rational perspective and cultivating a positive mindset.
    - **Result**: Reduced stress and increased mental resilience.

■

By incorporating these strategies into your daily life, you empower yourself to navigate stressors with grace and resilience. Embrace these practices, and let them serve as pillars of strength as you work towards a life filled with vitality and balance.

### - Ongoing preventative medical care and checkups

Ongoing preventative medical care and checkups are essential components of maintaining one's health and well-being. Regular visits to healthcare professionals, such as primary care physicians, specialists, and dentists, play a crucial role in preventing and identifying potential health issues before they escalate.

These routine checkups encompass a spectrum of services, including physical examinations, vaccinations, screenings, and diagnostic tests. By proactively engaging in preventative care, individuals not only take charge of their health but also empower themselves to make informed decisions for a healthier and more resilient future.

Wellbeing requires holistically addressing your physical, mental and social health. Pursue evidence-based habits promoting longevity, vigor and joy. You only get one body and mind – care for them diligently!

## CHAPTER 6: MANAGE YOUR FINANCES WISELY

"Too many people spend money they haven't earned, to buy things they don't want, to impress people they don't like." — Will Smith

In the pursuit of your ideal lifestyle, achieving financial stability is paramount. Taking control of your finances is key to this mastery. This chapter delves into principles for prudent spending, debt reduction, sufficient saving, and wealth building.

**- Steps for building an emergency fund and avoiding high-interest debt**
Commence with these foundational steps:

- **Create a Budget:** Track your income and expenses to gain a comprehensive understanding of where your money is going.

  **Example**: Consider using budgeting apps like Mint or YNAB to track every dollar you spend. Identify areas where you can cut back or allocate more funds based on your priorities.

- **Establish an Emergency Fund:** Safeguard yourself against unforeseen circumstances by having an emergency fund covering 3-6 months of expenses.

Example: Imagine unexpectedly losing your job or facing a medical emergency. Having an emergency fund of 3-6 months' worth of living expenses provides a financial safety net during challenging times.

- **Eliminate High-Interest Debt:** Prioritize paying off high-interest credit cards and other debts that drain your financial resources.

    Example: If you have credit card debt with high-interest rates, focus on paying it off aggressively. Allocate extra funds to the debt with the highest interest rate first while making minimum payments on others.

- **Intentional Spending:** Spend deliberately on priorities and values rather than succumbing to the allure of status or impulse purchases.

    Example: Instead of buying the latest gadget for status, consider whether it aligns with your values and long-term goals. Opt for purchases that contribute to your well-being and purpose.

- **Automate Savings:** Set up automated savings for crucial goals like retirement, education, and travel. Out of sight, out of mind.

    Example: Set up automatic transfers to your savings account each month. This can include contributions to your retirement fund, an emergency fund, or a travel fund. Automation ensures consistency.

With these basics in place, you can progress towards financial freedom and fulfillment.

- **Techniques to save and invest for short and long-term goals**

Once your financial groundwork is secure, shift your focus to leveraging savings for growth through strategic investing.

- **Retirement Savings:** Save at least 10-15% of your income in retirement accounts such as 401k or IRA. Maximize contributions yearly.
  **Example:** If your employer offers a 401k with a matching contribution, take full advantage. For instance, if they match up to 5%, contribute at least 5% of your salary to maximize this benefit.

- **Compound Growth:** Allow compound growth to work its magic. Over time and with discipline, wealth is created.
  **Example**: Starting to invest in your 20s versus your 40s can significantly impact your wealth due to the power of compounding. The earlier you start, the more time your money has to grow.

Through diligent saving and judicious investing, your money becomes a tool that generates more wealth.

- **Basics of investing in stocks, bonds, real estate**
  - **Diversified Portfolio:** Learn the basics of investing and create a diversified portfolio. Consider index funds for broad exposure.
    **Example:** Consider diversifying your investments by allocating funds to a mix of stocks, bonds, and real estate. Index funds can provide broad exposure to the stock market.

  - **Income-Generating Assets:** Invest in assets that produce ongoing income, such as rental property, dividend stocks, or a business.
    **Example:** Investing in dividend-paying stocks or a rental property can provide a steady stream of passive income, contributing to long-term financial stability.

- **Reducing expenses through minimalism and avoiding lifestyle inflation**

Adopt a discerning and intentional approach to purchasing, aligning your choices with what matters most. Embrace minimalism, only acquiring items that add genuine value. Curb spontaneous shopping and impulse buys.Exercise discernment in your spending by asking critical questions:

> **Purposeful Purchases:** Will this purchase align with my purpose and goals?
> **Example**: Before making a purchase, consider whether it aligns with your life goals. If you're saving

for a dream vacation, spending on non-essential items might hinder your progress.

➢ **Cost-Effective Alternatives:** Is there a less expensive alternative that meets the need? **Example**: Instead of buying a brand-new item, explore second-hand options or wait for sales. You might find cost-effective alternatives without compromising quality.

➢ **Value Over Status:** Am I buying for status or genuine happiness and comfort?
**Example**: Rather than purchasing a luxury item solely for its brand name, focus on items that genuinely enhance your daily life. Quality and utility should outweigh the desire for status.

- **Tools for tracking net worth over time**
Here are some tools you can use to track your net worth over time:

- **Personal Finance Apps:**
    - **Mint:** Mint is a popular personal finance app that allows you to link your bank accounts, credit cards, and investments. It provides a comprehensive overview of your financial situation, including your net worth.
    - **YNAB (You Need A Budget):** YNAB is a budgeting app that also tracks your net worth. It emphasizes a zero-based budgeting approach,

helping you allocate every dollar to a specific purpose.
- **Personal Capital:** This app offers tools for budgeting, investing, and tracking your net worth. It also provides a retirement planner and investment fee analyzer.

- **Excel or Google Sheets:**
  - Creating a simple spreadsheet in Excel or Google Sheets can be an effective way to track your net worth. List all your assets and liabilities, and update the sheet regularly.
  - You can find pre-made templates online for tracking net worth in spreadsheet format.

- **Financial Institutions' Platforms:**
  - Many banks and investment platforms offer tools to track your net worth within their platforms. Check if your financial institutions provide such features.

- **Net Worth Calculator Websites:**
  - Websites like Bankrate or NerdWallet offer net worth calculators. You input your assets and liabilities, and they calculate your net worth.

➤ **Quicken:**

- Quicken is a comprehensive personal finance software that allows you to track your net worth, create budgets, and manage your investments.

- **Wealth Management Platforms:**
  - Platforms like Wealthfront or Betterment not only manage your investments but also provide tools to track your overall financial picture, including net worth.

When choosing a tool, consider factors such as security, ease of use, and the specific features that matter most to you. Regularly updating your net worth is a valuable practice for understanding your financial progress and making informed decisions about your money.

By incorporating these principles and examples into your financial habits, you can gain control over your money, achieve your financial goals, and live a life aligned with your values. Mastering your finances is a journey toward empowerment and fulfillment.

## CHAPTER 7: TRAVEL AND EXPAND YOUR HORIZONS

Travel expands the spirit and offers a break from routine. It reminds you how big and amazing the world is. Seek new sights, meet new souls, and grow.

"Travel is the only thing you buy that makes you richer." – Anonymous

Experiencing new places and cultures expands perspective and fosters growth. This chapter reveals how to incorporate meaningful travel into your best life.

**- Benefits of travel like learning, relationships, mental health**
Embarking on a journey goes beyond the thrill of exploration—it's a conduit for personal growth and enriched well-being. Here are some key perks that make travel an invaluable asset:

- **Fresh Perspective:**
    - **Escape the Daily Routine:** Break free from the monotony of daily life to gain a fresh, invigorating perspective on the world.

Result: Renewed clarity and a broader outlook on life.

- **Cultural Immersion:**
    - **Learn About Diversity:** Immerse yourself in diverse cultures, histories, arts, and cuisines different from your own.
    Result: Expanded knowledge and a deep appreciation for global diversity.

- **Creating Lasting Memories:**
    - **Memorable Experiences:** Forge unforgettable moments with loved ones, creating a treasure trove of shared memories.
    Result: Strengthened bonds and a tapestry of cherished experiences.

- **Connecting with Others:**
    - **Global Connections:** Engage with locals and fellow travelers, building meaningful connections that transcend geographical boundaries.
    Result: A network of diverse friendships and a sense of global unity.

- **Mental Wellbeing Boost:**

- **Awe, Fun, Presence**: Experience the awe of breathtaking landscapes, the joy of new adventures, and the profound presence that travel brings.
  **Result**: Enhanced mental well-being and a rejuvenated spirit.

Whether you're jet-setting to far-off lands, embarking on a road trip, or finding solace in nature, every journey is a catalyst for personal transformation. Let the wings of travel carry you to new horizons, and let the world be your classroom for life's most impactful lessons.

- **Mastering the Art of Travel Logistics: Your Passport to Seamless Adventures**

Embarking on an adventure is an exhilarating prospect, but the magic lies in the meticulous planning that ensures a seamless journey. Here's your roadmap for mastering travel logistics:

- **Booking Essentials:**
  - **Flights and Lodging:** Secure your flights and lodging well in advance to snag the best deals and ensure availability.

- Hotel Selection: Read reviews to cherry-pick hotels that align with your preferences for comfort, amenities, and local charm.

- **Local Experiences:**
  - **Unique Tours:** Consider immersive tours, like a cooking class with a local chef, for exclusive access to the essence of the destination.
  - **Diverse Itinerary:** Plan an itinerary that strikes a balance between vibrant cities, breathtaking natural sites, and moments of tranquil downtime.

- **Road Trip Wisdom:**
  - **Key Stops:** For road trips, pinpoint a few key stops that offer a blend of planned activities and room for spontaneous discoveries.
  - **Camping Adventures:** Opt for camping to embrace a back-to-nature immersion, adding a touch of rustic charm to your journey.

Remember, logistics aren't just about practicality; they're the invisible threads weaving together a tapestry of unforgettable moments. So, as you plan your next adventure, let logistics be your trusted companion, enabling you to savor every moment of the remarkable journey that lies ahead.

- **Effortless Packing: Unleashing the Power of Checklists and Capsule Wardrobes**

Packing for a journey can be either a chaotic scramble or a well-choreographed dance. To transform your packing experience into a seamless affair, consider the two game-changing strategies: checklists and the capsule wardrobe approach.

**Checklist Mastery:**

- **Essentials First:**
    - Start with the essentials: passports, tickets, and any crucial travel documents. Ensure they are safely stowed in a designated travel wallet.

- **Clothing Strategy:**
    - Plan outfits day by day, considering the climate and activities. Versatile pieces that can be mixed and matched are your best allies.

- **Toiletries and Medications:**
    - Create a comprehensive list of toiletries and medications, ensuring you have everything you need for health and hygiene.

- **Gadgets and Chargers:**
  - List all electronic gadgets and their chargers. Prioritize based on importance, and ensure all necessary adapters are packed.
- **Emergency Kit:**
  - Assemble a compact emergency kit with items like a basic first aid set, a sewing kit, and a multi-tool.
- **Entertainment and Snacks:**
  - Include entertainment items, such as a book or e-reader, and snacks for the journey.

## Capsule Wardrobe Brilliance:

- **Mix-and-Match Pieces:**
  - Choose a color scheme that allows for easy mix-and-match. This minimizes the number of clothing items while maximizing outfit options.
- **Neutral Tones:**
  - Opt for neutral tones for your base items (like pants and jackets) to provide a versatile canvas for different looks.
- **Layering Magic:**
  - Embrace layering. A few well-chosen layers can adapt your outfit to various temperatures.

- **Accessories:**
    - Elevate your looks with accessories like scarves and jewelry, which take up minimal space but can transform an outfit.
- **Shoes with Purpose:**
    - Limit shoes to a few pairs that serve multiple purposes. For instance, comfortable walking shoes that also complement your evening attire.

By combining the precision of checklists with the efficiency of a capsule wardrobe, you're not just packing; you're orchestrating a symphony of travel-ready elements. As you zip up your suitcase, revel in the confidence of knowing that you've mastered the art of packing, setting the stage for a journey where every item is a purposeful note in the melody of your adventure.

- Types of trips from weekend getaways to long-term adventures

Embarking on a journey is not just about reaching a destination; it's about orchestrating an experience that resonates with your soul. Here's how you can compose the perfect symphony of discovery:

**Conducting Preliminary Research:**

- **Friendly Notes:**

Seek recommendations from friends and fellow travelers who have ventured to your chosen destination. Personal insights often unveil hidden treasures.

- **Expert Guidance:**

Delve into curated lists by travel experts. Online resources and guidebooks provide valuable insights into must-see attractions and off-the-beaten-path wonders.

- **Passion Points:**

Consider your passions and interests. Whether it's art, hiking, surfings, or history, align your activities with what sets your soul on fire.

**Navigating Beyond Tourist Trails:**

- **Local Insights:**

Connect with locals or explore online forums to discover authentic, local haunts. These gems often lie just beyond the tourist traps.

- **Wanderlust Philosophy:**

Embrace the philosophy of leaving room for serendipity. Some of the most cherished experiences unfold when you allow yourself to wander and discover spontaneously.

**Composition of Your Travel Symphony:**

- **Must-See Crescendos:**

Identify the must-see attractions that form the crescendos

of your journey. These landmarks could be iconic monuments, breathtaking landscapes, or culturally rich sites.

➤ **Harmony of Hidden Gems:**

Balance your itinerary with the harmony of hidden gems. These are the lesser-known spots that carry an air of mystery and authenticity.

➤ **Passionate Interludes:**

Insert activities aligned with your passions as interludes in your travel score. If you love art, visit local galleries; if history beckons, explore museums and historical sites.

➤ **Improvisational Spontaneity:**

Lastly, leave spaces in your itinerary for improvisation. Serendipitous encounters, unplanned detours, and unexpected discoveries often become the unforgettable notes in your travel composition.

As you meticulously plan your journey, envision it as a symphony where each activity, each sight, and each moment contribute to the masterpiece of your travel adventure. Let the conductor within you guide the way, creating a harmonious blend of planned precision and spontaneous crescendos.

- **Capturing memories and curios through journaling and photos**

A well-traveled heart is a treasury of memories, and the art lies in making those memories timeless. Here's how you can weave the magic to ensure your travels last far beyond the trip:

**Capturing the Essence Through Lens and Pen:**

> **Photographic Chronicles:**

Freeze moments in time with photographs that encapsulate the essence of each place. Capture not only landmarks but also the fleeting glances, vibrant markets, and everyday scenes that breathe life into your memories.

> **Journaling Adventures:**

Chronicle your journey through the art of journaling. Document not only the grand adventures but also the amusing mishaps, impactful encounters, and the spectrum of emotions each place evoked in you.

**Mementos that Echo Stories:**

> **Token Treasures:**

Select mementos that tell stories. It could be a ticket from a spontaneous train ride, pressed flowers from a quaint garden, or a small artisan gift that caught your eye. Each item becomes a portal to a specific memory.

> **Beyond the Fancy:**

Souvenirs need not be lavish or extravagant. The beauty lies in the simplicity of the touch – a seashell from a coastal walk, a handwritten note from a local friend, or a local delicacy that became your travel companion. It's the small, heartfelt touches that make journeys endure.

## A Symphony of Reminiscence:

> **Assembling the Memory Symphony:**

Imagine your memories as musical notes in a symphony. Your photographs, journal entries, and selected mementos harmonize to create a composition that resonates with the soul.

> **Journey Echoing Through Time:**

When you flip through the pages of your travel journal or glance at a framed photograph, the journey echoes through time. It's not just about the places you visited; it's about the emotions, stories, and personal growth woven into each step.

## Simple Touches, Timeless Journeys:

> **Essence of Everlasting Travel:**

In the end, it's the simple touches that transform travels into timeless journeys. The laughter shared with a stranger, the scent of a bustling market, the feeling of the wind on a mountaintop – these are the intangible souvenirs that stay with you forever.

> ### Crafting Your Legacy:

As you craft this legacy of memories, remember that the beauty of travel lies not just in the destinations but in the profound impact each journey leaves on your soul. May your adventures always echo in the symphony of your life.

# CHAPTER 8: MAKE TIME FOR WHAT MATTERS

"Time is really the only capital that any human being has and the thing that he can least afford to waste or lose." – Thomas Edison

With life's demands, it's easy to become too busy to focus on priorities. Mastering your time enables you to deliberately spend it on what matters most. This chapter reveals how to reclaim your calendar and schedule purposefully.

**- Identifying top priorities in your life**
Embarking on the journey to your best life begins with the clarity of purpose. Across the vast landscape of life, let's define the guiding stars that will light your path:

➤ **Relationships – Nurturing Bonds:**
   Top Priorities:
   - Quality time with spouse
   - Engaging dates with kids

- **Health – A Commitment to Well-being:**
  Top Priorities:
  - Consistent gym sessions
  - Dedicated time for meal prep

- **Learning – Fueling Growth:**
  Top Priorities:
  - Skill building through online courses
  - Devoted time to reading and expanding knowledge

- **Recreation – Balancing Life's Symphony:**
  Top Priorities:
  - Invigorating hikes on weekends
  - Monthly self-care through rejuvenating massages

- **Passions – Igniting the Soul:**
  Top Priorities:
  - Artistic fulfillment through photography editing
  - Contributing to the community via volunteering at an animal shelter

With the tapestry of your priorities laid out, remember this cardinal rule: schedule them first before anything else. By anchoring your schedule around these priorities, you not only honor your commitments but also sow the seeds for a life deeply rooted in purpose and fulfillment. This intentional approach ensures that your journey aligns with the destinations that truly matter.

**- Reducing time on activities that drain energy**
In the quest for your best life, the liberation of time becomes a formidable ally. Here's your roadmap to freeing up precious moments by strategically minimizing time drains:

> **Social Media and Web Browsing Detox:**

   **Strategy:**

   - Set specific time slots for social media.
   - Unsubscribe from unnecessary email lists.
   - Utilize website blockers during focused work hours.

> **Streamlined Entertainment Consumption:**

   **Strategy:**

   - Opt for intentional viewing.
   - Designate specific days for binge-watching.
   - Explore alternative leisure activities.

> **Thoughtful Shopping Ventures:**

   **Strategy:**

   - Embrace mindful shopping lists.
   - Leverage online shopping to save time.
   - Plan efficient shopping routes to minimize travel time.

> **Commute Optimization (For Remote Workers):**

**Strategy:**

- ❖ Negotiate remote work days.
- ❖ Utilize commuting time for personal growth (podcasts, audiobooks).
- ❖ Implement flexible work hours for increased efficiency.

By selectively pruning activities that devour your time, you create spaciousness for the blossoming of your priorities. Embrace this liberation with purpose, as every freed-up minute becomes an investment in your journey towards a life well-lived.

## - Scheduling techniques like time blocking to focus on priorities

Unlock the potential of your daily or weekly calendar by adopting the art of time blocking. Here's your tailored strategy to infuse your schedule with the essence of your top priorities:

> **Dedicated Time Slots:**

**Strategy:**

- ❖ Allocate 1-2-hour blocks for your pivotal priorities.
- ❖ Reserve specific days for particular activities.

➤ **Peak Energy Precision:**

**Strategy:**

- ❖ Identify your peak energy periods (morning, afternoon).
- ❖ Schedule high-focus tasks during these energy peaks.

➤ **Full Immersion Days:**

**Strategy:**

- ❖ Designate entire days for specific pursuits.
- ❖ Create an environment free from competing engagements.

➤ **Task Clustering Brilliance:**

**Strategy:**

- ❖ Group similar tasks for streamlined efficiency.
- ❖ Tackle errands in a single, time-efficient cluster.
- ❖ Harnessing the Power of Scheduled Priorities

Through meticulous time blocking, your calendar transforms into a dynamic canvas, painted with the vibrant hues of your priorities. Embrace the structure, relish the focus, and watch as your best life

unfolds within the carefully crafted contours of your daily rhythm.

- **Practicing saying no to nonessential requests and commitments**

In the quest for a life of intention and meaning, the sacredness of your time must be defended. Here's your manifesto to fortify your time fortress:

1. **Sentinels of Focus:**

    Declaration:

    ❖ Guard protected time blocks with unwavering commitment.
    ❖ Treat them with the reverence accorded to crucial appointments.

2. **Unyielding No:**

    Declaration:

    ❖ Embrace the liberating power of saying no to conflicting demands.
    ❖ Prioritize your purpose over the allure of immediate distractions.

3. **Deliberate Living Pledge:**

    Declaration:

    ❖ Pledge to be deliberate in every minute and hour.

❖ Let your daily priorities be the architects of your lifelong goals.

In the relentless pursuit of purposeful living, you stand as the guardian of your most precious resource—time. With every resolute 'no' and vigilant protection of your time blocks, you fortify the foundation of a life that aligns with your deepest aspirations. Embrace the power to guard, defend, and ultimately thrive.

## CHAPTER 9: DISCOVER WORK YOU LOVE

"Choose a job you love, and you will never have to work a day in your life." - Confucius

Work occupies much of life. Ensuring it aligns with your passion and purpose is key to living your best life. This chapter reveals how to find or create work you find genuinely meaningful.

- **Reflecting on skills, interests and values to identify ideal work**
Embarking on a journey to discover your ideal work is akin to navigating the labyrinth of self-awareness. Consider this as your personal odyssey, a map to unleash your professional passion:

- ➤ **The Reflective Compass:**
  - o **Assessment Ritual:**
    - Reflect on your skills, interests, values, and personality traits.
    - Unearth the compass within, pointing toward work that resonates with your essence.
- ➤ **Past Echoes:**
  - o **Investigative Quest:**
    - Delve into your professional history.
    - Examine jobs that ignited your passion versus those that left you yearning for escape. Seek the common threads weaving through these experiences.
- ➤ **Passionate Dialogues:**
  - o **Inner Conversations:**
    - Engage in deep introspection.
    - Explore the topics that set your soul on fire, the subjects you eagerly read about and discuss. Uncover the whispers of your vocational calling.
- ➤ **Imaginary Freedom:**
  - o **Fantasy Exploration:**
    - Envision a reality where financial concerns are irrelevant.
    - What would you choose to do in this utopian realm? This fantasy holds the key to your heart's professional desire.

- **The Symbiotic Harmony:**
  - **Ideal Work Ecosystem:**
    - Seek the sweet spot where your skills meet your passions.
    - The ideal work environment is a harmonious echo of your authentic self.

In the symphony of your professional life, each note is a manifestation of your skills, passions, and purpose. The score is written by your experiences and aspirations. Embrace the odyssey, decode the music within, and let it guide you to the work that harmonizes with your very being.

**- Considering side hustles, entrepreneurship, or career change**
Embarking on the entrepreneurial odyssey offers a symphony of freedoms, each note echoing the benefits of owning a small business:

- **Conducting Your Time:**
  - **Autonomy Awaits:**
    - Seize control of your schedule, orchestrating the rhythm of your work-life balance.
    - Flexibility becomes the maestro, allowing you to synchronize work with life's diverse movements.

- ➢ **The Canvas of Creativity:**
  - o **Expressive Flourish:**
    - Unleash your creativity on a grand scale.
    - As the artistic director of your enterprise, every stroke of innovation contributes to the masterpiece of your vision.

- ➢ **Impactful Crescendo:**
  - o **Direct Influence:**
    - Stand at the podium of influence, conducting change through your work.
    - The impact of your efforts resounds directly, reaching the ears of those your business touches.

- ➢ **The Blueprint Prelude:**
  - o **Strategic Composition:**
    - Before the grand performance, compose a business plan that harmonizes your vision with practicality.
    - Outline your services, orchestrate startup costs, set the pricing tempo, and identify the audience your symphony aims to enrapture.

Owning a small business is not just a venture; it's a symphony of freedom, creativity, and impact. As you wield the conductor's baton, let the music of your passion and expertise resound in every entrepreneurial note.

**- Steps for launching a new business doing work you enjoy**
In the grand orchestration of your current career, there are subtle yet powerful movements that can elevate your work experience. Here's a score for optimizing your current role:

- **Harmonize Interests with Duties:**
  - **Artful Alignment:**
    - Discover the resonant frequencies between your interests and your role.
    - Seek opportunities to infuse your daily duties with the melody of your passions.

- **Cultivate a Melodic Connection:**
  - **Collegial Crescendo:**
    - Forge connections with colleagues whose energy harmonizes with yours.
    - In the workplace symphony, collaborative notes create a harmonious ambiance.

- Virtuoso Volunteerism:
  - Purposeful Projects:
    - Volunteer for projects that align with your strengths and purpose.
    - Let your contribution be a virtuoso performance, showcasing the brilliance of your capabilities.

While a change of careers might not be on the immediate horizon, the current professional stage offers ample room for refinement. By aligning your duties with your interests, fostering connections, and engaging in purposeful projects, you transform the daily grind into a symphony of fulfillment and growth.


- Finding fulfillment in current work through relationships and impact

In the vast terrain of your professional journey, strategic navigation and intentional connections becomes the compass guiding you toward fulfillment. Here's your map to chart this course:

- Connective Bridges:
  - Professional Alliances:
    - Join related professional groups to forge connections and share insights.
    - Networking within these alliances constructs bridges that traverse the professional landscape.

- **Expression of Talents:**
  - **Artful Imperfection:**
    - Look for opportunities to express your talents and make a difference through your work, even in imperfect ways.
    - Progressing toward purpose doesn't demand perfection; it evolves in stages.

- **The Right Work Symphony:**
  - **Harmony in Stages:**
    - Your work, like a symphony, plays an oversized role in your fulfillment.
    - Seek work that aligns with your passions, creating a harmonious flow that resonates with your purpose.

Embark on this professional odyssey with intentional connections, expressions of your talents, and a keen sense of purpose. As you navigate this landscape, remember: the right work, whether by change or redesign, is a pivotal chord in the symphony of living your best life.

## CONCLUSION

The journey to your best life is an ever-unfolding process versus a single destination. By applying the principles in this book, you now have the roadmap to consciously design a life of passion, purpose and fulfilment.

The first step is self-discovery – unearthing your core passions, values, and sense of purpose. With clarity on your own truth, you can set goals and priorities aligned with who you authentically are. Develop and nurture supportive daily habits and rituals. Foster relationships that energize you. Care for your physical and mental health with diligence. Manage your finances wisely to enable pursuing your dreams.

While each day will have challenges, maintain perspective. With the right mindset and consistent practice, you grow stronger, wiser, and more empowered to live out our purpose. Lean on the tools and techniques that work for you. Have patience with yourself as you progress one step at a time.

Trust in your capacity to create positive change. Believe you deserve to thrive across all of life's domains. Uplift others through generosity of spirit as you learn and evolve. Fulfillment is not a permanent state, but an ongoing process of mindfully experiencing each moment.

You now hold the keys needed to awaken your best life.

**- Review of techniques and principles covered**
As we conclude our journey through the principles of living your best life, let's revisit the key waypoints that guide you toward fulfilment:

- **Self-Discovery Voyage:**
  - *Unearth your passions and purpose through deep self-reflection.*
  - *This foundational step sets the course for a purposeful life.*

- **Navigating Goals:**
  - *Craft S.M.A.R.T. goals that align with your purpose.*
  - *Regularly track your progress, ensuring you stay on course toward your aspirations.*

- **Habits and Rituals:**
  - *Foster supportive habits and rituals while guarding against distractions.*
  - *These routines become the pillars that sustain your journey.*

- **Relationship Resonance:**
  - *Deepen connections with relationships that energize and uplift you.*
  - *Create a network of positive influences that amplify your growth.*

- **Body and Mind Harmony:**
  - *Care for your body through mindful nutrition, fitness, quality sleep, and stress management.*

- *Achieve holistic well-being for sustained vitality.*

➢ **Financial Fortitude:**
- *Steward your finances consciously – save, invest, and spend with purpose.*
- *Financial stability forms a solid foundation for a fulfilling life.*

➢ **Travel as Transformation:**
- *Explore new horizons through travel to reignite your passion for life.*
- *Discover the transformative power of immersing yourself in diverse experiences.*

➢ **Time Mastery:**
- *Deliberately schedule priorities, minimizing time drains.*
- *Be the architect of your time, ensuring that it aligns with your deepest values.*

➢ **Purposeful Work:**
- *Seek work that utilizes your strengths and aligns with your sense of purpose.*
- *Your professional journey is a significant part of your life's symphony.*

➢ **Common Threads:**
- *Self-awareness, intentionality, balance, and nurturing growth across all life domains weave these principles together.*

- *Mastery of even a few principles will propel you forward on your quest for a purposeful and fulfilling life.*

As you navigate the intricate tapestry of your existence, may these principles serve as guiding stars, illuminating the path to your best life. Bon voyage!

### - Developing long-term vision for your best life
The journey to living your best life is an ever-evolving adventure. Regularly refine your vision for the future to ensure alignment with your deepest desires. Here's a blueprint for this ongoing process:

- **Periodic Reflections:**
  - Time Horizons: Envision life at 5, 10, 20+ years. Allow your vision to expand and adapt to changing circumstances.
  - Annual Reviews: Set aside time annually to reflect on your life's direction.

- **Emerging Passions:**
  - Inquiry: What new passions have emerged or evolved? Explore and embrace these emerging facets of yourself.

- **Accomplishments Acknowledgment:**
  - Celebration: Cross off accomplished goals. Celebrate achievements, and acknowledge the progress you've made.

- **Setting New Milestones:**
  - **Reassess Goals:** What new milestones can you set across various facets of life? Challenge yourself to aim higher.

- **Evolving Priorities and Relationships:**
  - **Dynamic Evaluation:** How have priorities and relationships evolved? Adapt to changing dynamics, nurturing what matters most.

- **Purposeful Realignment:**
  - **Purpose Check:** Does your purpose remain aligned and inspiring? Reconnect with your sense of purpose and adjust if needed.

- **Course Correction:**
  - **Flexibility:** A long-term vision provides a flexible framework. Be open to course corrections as you gain new insights and experiences.

- **Reaching Highest Potential:**
  - **Continuous Growth:** Continually reach for your highest potential. Embrace a growth mindset that propels you forward.

Your life's vision is a living document, reflecting the dynamic essence of who you are and who you aspire to become. By engaging in this ongoing process, you empower yourself to live a life that is both intentional and deeply fulfilling. Keep reaching for the stars!

## - Navigating Life's Twists: A Guide to Adaptation and Growth

Life is a dynamic journey, and embracing change is key to sustained fulfillment. Here's a guide to navigate life's twists with resilience and purpose:

> **Reflect on Major Life Events:**
>   - **Pause and Assess:** During significant life events, reflect on how they impact your purpose. Adjust goals to align with your evolving vision.

> **Break Free from Routines:**
>   - **Shake Things Up:** If you find yourself in a rut, break free from routines. Travel, learn something new, or meet people who inspire fresh perspectives.

> **Actively Make Time for Priorities:**
>   - **Proactive Adjustment:** As priorities evolve, actively make time for what now matters

most. Be intentional about aligning your actions with your current values.

- ➢ **Adapt Techniques to Your Evolution:**
    - **Embrace Change:** If certain techniques no longer serve you, embrace change. Try new approaches that align with the person you've become on your journey.

Life is an ever-changing canvas, and your ability to adapt and grow is a testament to your resilience. Embrace each twist and turn, viewing them as opportunities for self-discovery and growth. As you navigate the unknown, remember that every step contributes to the masterpiece of your unique and purposeful life.

- Navigating Storms: Strategies for Difficult Days

Life's storms are inevitable, but your ability to navigate them is a testament to your resilience. Here are strategies to weather difficult days:

- ➢ **Daily Gratitude Journaling:**
    - **Reflect and Appreciate:** Take a moment each day to journal your blessings and achievements. Gratitude grounds you in positivity.

- ➢ **Revisit Your Purpose and Vision:**
  - **Anchor in "Why":** When the storm clouds gather, revisit your purpose and vision. Remembering your "why" provides clarity and motivation.

- ➢ **Consume Inspiring Content:**
  - **Nourish Your Soul:** Immerse yourself in inspiring content—books, podcasts, nature. Fuel your mind and spirit with positivity.

- ➢ **Limit Exposure to Negativity:**
  - **Guard Your Peace:** Minimize exposure to negative news and people. Protect your mental and emotional well-being.

- ➢ **Maintain Supportive Connections:**
  - **Lean on Others:** Stay connected with supportive friends and family. Sharing burdens lightens the load.

- ➢ **Believe in Your Ability:**
  - **Inner Resilience:** Cultivate belief in your ability to overcome obstacles. Trust in your strength and resilience.

- **Take Action:**
  - **Progress Fuels Motivation:** Even small steps count. Take action, as progress fuels motivation and propels you forward.

With consistent practice, these principles for designing your best life become ingrained habits. In the face of adversity, you'll find strength, purpose, and the resilience to navigate storms.

- **The Final Thoughts**

In the tapestry of life, each thread represents a choice, a decision, a moment of intention. As we conclude this journey together, remember that designing your best life is an ongoing, dynamic process. The principles and techniques shared serve as tools in your toolkit, ready to be wielded with purpose.

Embrace the power of self-awareness, intentionality, and balance. Discover your passions, set goals that align with your purpose, cultivate supportive habits, and nurture meaningful relationships. Your journey is unique, and each step, whether large or small, contributes to the masterpiece that is your life.

In the face of challenges, storms, and uncertainties, you possess the resilience to weather them. On difficult days, recall your purpose, practice gratitude, and take intentional steps forward. Your potential is boundless, and your ability to shape a life of fulfillment and meaning is within your hands.

As you navigate the currents of time, continually revisit your vision, adjust your sails, and adapt to the evolving landscape of your aspirations. Life is a canvas waiting for the strokes of your choices.

May you live with intention, embrace growth, and savor the richness of each moment. Here's to crafting and living your best life.

# ABOUT THE AUTHOR

Dear readers!

Let me introduce myself – I'm not your typical author, not by a long shot. In the daylight hours, I'm the resident computer science whiz, cracking codes and navigating digital realms. But when the stars take their place in the night sky, I transform into a loving mother, a storyteller, and a passionate writer.

My heart's true calling is found in the written word. I've embarked on a mission, you see. It's a mission to weave the virtues of kindness, compassion, and love into the very fabric of young minds, and I've chosen the enchanting realm of children's books as my vessel.

But hold on, our journey doesn't end there. I'm here to light a fire within adults too. In the pages of my self-help books, you'll find the keys to personal growth, motivation, and inspiration.

So, I invite you to join me. Together, we'll set sail on a literary adventure, where words become bridges between generations, and where the magic of storytelling sparks transformative change. Welcome to a world where the ordinary transforms into the extraordinary, where potential knows no bounds, and where the power of words is the catalyst for profound, positive shifts.

Printed in Great Britain
by Amazon